TRIVIA AMERICANA

Pop Culture, Military History, State Facts, & Much More

By Whiskey Hamilton

TRIVIA AMERICANA

the information contained within this document, including, but not limited to, — errors, omissions, or inaccuracies.

ISBN: 978-1-961887-01-5

Trivia Americana

Pop Culture, Military History, State
Facts, & Much More

Whiskey Hamilton

Valhalla Industries LLC

Contents

Chapter One

American Presidents

Q : Which U.S. President had to have the White House fitted with a much larger bathtub?
A: William Howard Taft

Q: Which U.S. President is associated with the March of Dimes?
A: Franklin D. Roosevelt

Q: Which presidential candidate signed the Declaration of Independence before becoming the second elected President of the United States?
A: John Adams

Q: Who was the U.S. President who held office at the beginning of the Korean War?
A: Harry S. Truman

Q: Which signers of the Declaration of Independence would reach the office of President of the United States?

A: Thomas Jefferson and John Adams

Q: How many U.S. Presidents are veterans?

A: 31

Q: Mount Vernon Plantation is named after what famous British officer?

A: Admiral Edward Vernon

Q: The Bay of Pigs took place under which President?

A: John F. Kennedy

Q. Who was the U.S. President responsible for creating the Secret Service?

A: Abraham Lincoln

Q: Which future U.S. President was shot down in aerial combat?

A: George H.W. Bush

Q: Which U.S. President first served as Minister to Russia?

A: James Buchanan

Q: Who was the first U.S. President to die while serving his elected term?

A: William Henry Harrison

Q: At the Battle of Buena Vista, which future U.S. President defeated General Antonio López de Santa Anna?

A: Zachary Taylor

Q: Which U.S. President worked as a teacher prior to pursuing politics?

A: Lyndon B. Johnson

Q: Which U.S. President later served as an elected representative to the Confederacy?

A: John Tyler

Q: Who was nicknamed "The Little Magician"?

A: Martin Van Buren

Q: Which U.S. Presidents received the Nobel Peace Prize?

A: Woodrow Wilson, Jimmy Carter, and Barack Obama

Q: Which U.S. President commissioned the first modern warships?

A: Benjamin Harrison

Q: The Teapot Dome Scandal occurred under which administration?

A: Warren G. Harding

Q: Which U.S. President held the nickname "Old Hickory"?

A: Andrew Jackson

Q: The Kansas-Nebraska Act was passed during which presidency?

A: Franklin Pierce

Q: Who was the U.S. President responsible for Operation Warp Speed?

A: Donald J. Trump

Q: True or false? Rutherford B. Hayes vetoed the Chinese Exclusion Act.

A: True

Q: Besides Abraham Lincoln and John F. Kennedy, which two U.S. Presidents were assassinated in office?

A: James A. Garfield & William McKinley

Q: Who was known as the "Conservation President"?

A: Theodore Roosevelt

Q: The Respect for Marriage Act was signed by which president?

A: Joseph Biden

Q: During the American Civil War, which future U.S. President served as a Quartermaster for the State of New York?

A: Chester A. Arthur

Q: Which President declared war on Terror?

A: George W. Bush

Q: Who was the first U.S. President to meet an Emperor of Japan?

A: Ulysses S. Grant

Q: Who is the only U.S. President to ever personally carry out a public execution?

A: Grover Cleveland

Q: What former U.S. President changed his last name from Blythe?
A: William Clinton

Q: The Camp David Accords took place during which administration?
A: James Carter

Q: The Continental Congress boasted which future president as its youngest delegate?
A: James Madison

Q: Which former President spent seventeen years as a delegate in the House of Representatives after leaving office?
A: John Quincy Adams

Q: Fill in the blank of this past presidential running slogan: "Keep cool with _____."
A: Coolidge

Q: Which President welcomed home the crew of the Apollo XI?
A: Richard Nixon

Q: What was the name of Ronald Reagan's favorite cologne?
A: Royal Briar

Q: Which future U.S. President got caught in the Boxer Rebellion?
A: Herbert Hoover

Q: Which future U.S. President helped to negotiate the Louisiana Purchase?

A: James Monroe

Chapter Two

U.S. Sports

Q : Which legendary baseball player hit 714 home runs?
A: Babe Ruth

Q: In what city was the NFL founded?
A: Canton, Ohio

Q: The Negro National League was formed in what year?
A:1920

Q: In the 1950-1951 season, who lost the NBA Championship to the Rochester Royals?
A: New York Knickerbockers

Q: Before they changed their name, the Tennessee Titans were known as?
A: Tennessee Oilers

Q: In 1917, the NHL was organized after the suspension of operations of what league?

A: National Hockey Association of Canada Limited (NHA)

Q: The Belmont was won by what horse in 2015?

A: American Pharaoh

Q: In 1999, 2003, 2005, 2007, and 2014, what was the name of the coach who led the San Antonio Spurs to the NBA Championship?

A: Gregg Popovich

Q: When considering a name for the Minnesota Vikings, which name was not officially considered as an option: the Chippewas, Mariners, or the Voyageurs?

A: Mariners

Q: The New York Americans changed their name from the Brooklyn Americans during which season?

A: 1941-1942

Q: The Basketball Hall of Fame added which player in 2018?

A: Steve Nash

Q: The Women's National Soccer team won the Gold Cup in what year for the U.S. for the first time?

A: 1991

Q: In 1975, the name USTA was formally adopted by the league. What was it previously known as?

A: U.S. Lawn Tennis Association

Q: In 1962, what NBA player joined the Celtics after being cut from the Browns?

A: John Havlicek

Q: In what year did Secretariat run the fastest Kentucky Derby in history?

A: 1973

Q: In 1963, the International Tennis Federation's international women's team championship was won by the U.S. against what country?

A: Australia

Q: In 1965, Muhammad Ali defeated which boxer in a first-round knock-out victory?

A: Sonny Liston

Q: Who was the 2023 UFC Flyweight champion?
A: Alexa Grasso

Q: The 1962 Super Bowl was held in what city?
A: New York City

Q: In 2012, who won first place in the Open Division of the National Ranch Horse Association Championship?

A: Jennifer Keeney on Phantom Yankee

Q: Who won the Bareback Riding World Championship from 1971-1975?

A: Joe Alexander

Q: Tenley Albright was a survivor of childhood Polio and took the gold during the Cortina d'Ampezzo 1956 Olympic Winter Games. In what event was she competing?

A: Figure skating

Q: In 1996, Beach Volleyball was added as an event in the Summer Olympics. Where did this first competition take place?

A: Atlantic Beach

Q: Who was the first athlete in history to win an event in all six skiing disciplines: downhill, super-G, slalom, giant slalom, combined, and parallel?

A: Mikaela Shiffrin

Q: In 1983, the PGA tour started tracking holes-in-one. Which two players hold the record of 10?

A: Hal Sutton and Robert Allenby

Q: Who are the only two Nascar drivers who have won seven series championships?

A: Dale Earnhart and Richard Petty

Q: Sam Snead and Tiger Woods tied for the record number of wins in the PGA. How many career wins do they each hold?

A: 82

Q: The American Bowling Congress was first formed in 1985, at Beethoven Hall in New York City. Who served as the organization's first president?

A: Thomas Curtis

Q: When the Hart-Agnew Act of 1908 threatened to eradicate horse racing in the state of New York, what event kept the sport alive?

A: Steeplechasing

Q: Dick Plasman was the last football player to play a game in the NFL without a helmet. In what year did he play that last game without a helmet?

A: 1940

Q: In 1948, where was the first Nascar race held?

A: Daytona Beach, Florida

Q: In 1988, Florence Griffith Joyner, set records in what two track events?

A: 100-meter dash and 200-meter dash

Q: What group is recognized as the first soccer club to be organized in America?

A: The Oneidas of Boston

Q: In 1982, who was the only marksman the NSSA inducted into the Hall of Fame?

A: Ila Hill

Q: In 1996, the Women's National Soccer team defeated what country for the Olympic gold?

A: China

Q: Who pitched the last legal spitball?

A: Burleigh Grimes

Q: Who was the Bull Riding World Champion in 1951, and again from 1954-1959?

A: Jim Shoulders

Q: In how many U.S. cities was the 1994 Fifa World Cup Hosted?

A: 9

Q: What is the fastest record in Barrel Racing?

A: 13.46 seconds

Q: What NFL player holds the record for career touchdowns with 208?

A: Jerry Rice

Chapter Three

U.S. States

Q: What is the state flower of Connecticut?
A: Mountain Laurel

Q: What bird has been chosen as the official state bird of New Mexico? Hint: its scientific name is: Geococcyx californianus.
A: The Greater Roadrunner

Q: Standing a staggering 14,400 feet, what is the name of the tallest peak in Colorado?
A: Mount Elbert

Q: "Union, Justice, Confidence" is the motto of what state?
A: Louisiana

Q: What is the state fabric of California?
A: Denim

Q: Myakka fine sand has been chosen as the official soil of what state?

A: Florida

Q: The Garnet is the official gem of what state?

A: New York

Q: What is the state flower of Kansas?

A: The Wild Sunflower

Q: The Horned Lizard was chosen as the official reptile of what state?

A: Texas

Q: What drink is the official state drink in 21 states?

A: Milk

Q: The Four Corners Monument is in what four states?

A: Arizona, Utah, Colorado, and New Mexico

Q: The Duck-billed Dinosaur is the official fossil of what state?

A: Montana

Q: Which coastal state chose the Pink Lady's Slipper as its official flower?

A: New Hampshire

Q: What state chose the ice cream cone as its official dessert?

A: Missouri

Q: What is the official motto of the state of Ohio?
A: With God all things are possible

Q: The Chokecherry is the official fruit of what state?
A: North Dakota

Q: What is the state grape of Arkansas?
A: Cynthiana Grape

Q: What is the official state animal of Vermont?
A: Morgan Horse

Q: What insect has been chosen by sixteen states as the official insect?
A: Honey Bee

Q: The Hall Flintlock Model 1819 is the official firearm of what state?
A: West Virginia

Q: "Industry" is the official motto of what state?
A: Utah

Q: What tree did the state of Indiana choose as its official tree?
A: Tulip Poplar

Q: In what state is the American Alligator the official reptile?
A: Mississippi

Q: Which flower has the state of North Carolina chosen to be its official flower?

A: Dogwood

Q: What is the state nickname for New Jersey?

A: The Garden State

Q: In which state is the Eastern Goldfinch the official bird?

A: Iowa

Q: What game bird was chosen to be the official game bird of the state of Massachusetts?

A: Wild Turkey

Q: Which state chose the Black-capped Chickadee as its official bird?

A: Maine

Q: What is the official dog of Tennessee?

A: Blue Tick Coonhound

Q: What is the official state gospel song of Oklahoma?

A: Swing Low Sweet Chariot

Q: What is the state fleet of Virginia?

A: Jamestown Colonial Ships

Q: Which midwestern state is proclaimed to be "The Prairie State"?

A: Illinois

Q: What is the official tree of Washington state?

A: Western Hemlock

Q: Which state chose "North to the Future" as its official motto?

A: Alaska

Q: American Holly is the official tree of what state?

A: Delaware

Q: Black Coral is the official gem of what state?

A: Hawaii

Q: What is the state flagship of Pennsylvania?

A: U.S. Brig Niagara

Q: Which tree was chosen by the state of Michigan as its official tree?

A: Eastern White Pine

Q: Indian Ricegrass is the official grass in what state?

A: Nevada

Q: The state of Oregon chose what nut as its official nut?

A: Hazelnut

Q: What state has been nicknamed "the Ocean State"?

A: Rhode Island

Q: What is the state mammal of Wyoming?

A: American Bison

Chapter Four

U.S. Military History

Q: Benedict Arnold's infamous betrayal took place at what famous site?

A: West Point

Q: With an estimated 51,112 casualties, what battle took place in Adams County Pennsylvania?

A: Gettysburg

Q: Finish the phrase: "one if by land...."

A: Two if by sea

Q: Though omitted from Henry Wadsworth Longfellow's famous poem, who were the five night riders who carried the news that the British were coming?

A: Paul Revere, Samuel Prescott, Israel Bissell, William Dawes, and Sybil Ludington

Q: The ironclad vessel C.S.S. Virginia was originally what vessel?
A: U.S.S. Merrimack

Q: What famous communication was decrypted by British code breakers and ultimately led the U.S. into World War I?
A: Zimmerman Telegram

Q: Who was in command of Texas forces during the Battle of the Alamo?
A: William Barret Travis

Q: Where were the winter quarters of General George Washington in 1777?
A: Valley Forge

Q: In 1945, the U.S. dropped the atomic bomb on what two cities?
A: Hiroshima and Nagasaki

Q: Besides the World Trade Centers and the Pentagon, where else was a plane crashed on 9/11?
A: A field in Pennsylvania.

Q: Which invasion went by the code name Operation Overlord?
A: D-Day

Q: True or False? The Americans won the Battle of Bunker Hill.
A: False

Q: "The shot heard round the world" is a reference to what battle that began the American Revolution?

A: Lexington and Concord

Q: Who was in command of the United Nations Forces during the Korean War?

A: General Douglas A. MacArthur

Q: General James McPherson, the commander of the Tennessee Army, was killed in what battle of the Civil War?

A: Battle of Atlanta

Q: Where was the detention center called Guantanamo Bay set up?

A: Cuba

Q: During the Tunisia Campaign, while British forces captured the capital, what important port was the American forces capturing?

A: Bizerte

Q: Colonel William Prescott is famous for what quote before the Battle of Bunker Hill?

A: "Do not fire until you see the whites of their eyes!"

Q: The Civil War officially began in 1861, when what fort was fired upon?

A: Fort Sumter

Q: What Axis Power was the last to surrender to the Allies?

A: Japan

Q: Francis Scott Key was inspired to write the "Star Spangled Banner" while watching the bombardment of Fort Henry during what Battle?

A: Battle of Baltimore

Q: What military engagement was known as "The First Space War"?

A: Desert Storm

Q: True or False? The city of Savannah, Georgia was burned to the ground by General William Tecumseh Sherman during his infamous "March to the Sea"?

A: False

Q: In what country was Osama Bin Laden, finally found and killed by U.S. forces on May 1st, 2011?

A: Pakistan

Q: The Ho Chi Minh Trail passed through not only Vietnam, but what other two countries?

A: Laos and Cambodia

Q: In 1861, what city officially became the capital of the Confederacy?

A: Richmond

Q: What assault during the Vietnam War began with attacks on Hué and Saigon?

A: Tet Offensive

Q: In 1845, Annapolis Naval Academy was opened on the 10-acre site of what previous Army Fort?

A: Fort Severn

Q: Though the American Civil War began in 1861, in what year did the Emancipation Proclamation, signed by President Abraham Lincoln, go into effect?

A: 1863

Q: Name the victor of the last battle of the Civil War, fought at Palmito Ranch, Texas.

A: the Confederacy

Q: What division of the U.S. Navy was organized when the Navy Women's Reserve Act was signed into law by President Franklin Roosevelt?

A: Waves

Q: During the final Civil War battle to be fought in the Shenandoah Valley, who commanded the Confederate troops?

A: General Jubal Early

Q: Colonel Theodore Roosevelt organized and rode in a volunteer regiment of "Rough Riders" during what 10-week war?

A: The Spanish American War

Q: In what year did World War II end?
A: 1945

Q: True or False? Fort Pulaski was included on the list of Underground Railroad destinations.

A: True

Q: The British Army was commanded by which general during the American Revolution?

A: General Charles Cornwallis

Q: Following the attacks of September 11th, 2001, what was famously declared by President George W. Bush?

A: A War on Terror

Q: On D-Day, how many beaches were actually stormed by the Allied forces?

A: Five

Q: Where did the Confederate, ship the C.S.S. Shenandoah, surrender in 1865?

A: Liverpool, England

Q: True or False? The U.S. and Great Britain entered World War I at the same time.

A: False

Chapter Five

U.S. Geography and Topography

Q : Which river in the U.S. holds the title of the longest?

A: Missouri River

Q: The Appalachian Mountain range begins in Maine, in which southern state does it end?

A: Alabama

Q: What is the only Great Lake entirely encompassed by the United States?

A: Lake Michigan

Q: North of San Francisco, where is the first deep-water harbor?

A: The mouth of the Columbia River

Q: What is the most active volcano in the U.S. and the world?

A: Mount Kilauea

Q: Which state is home to the delta of the mighty Mississippi River?

A: Louisiana

Q: What U.S. Territory is home to El Yunque, the only tropical forest in the U.S. Forest Service?

A: Puerto Rico

Q: How many units does the National Parks System manage in the U.S.?

A: 424

Q: What mountain range is home to the tallest mountains in the U.S.?

A: Alaska Mountain Range

Q: The Potomac River flows into what bay?

A: The Chesapeake Bay

Q: Where was the first hydropower plant constructed in the United States?

A: Grand Rapids, Michigan

Q: Which mountain is the shortest classified mountain in the U.S.?

A: Britton Hill

Q: Flowing from the San Juan Mountains in Colorado, what river separates the United States from Mexico?

A: The Rio Grande River

Q: Which Great Lake is similar in surface dimensions to Lake Erie, but is much deeper?

A: Lake Ontario

Q: What mountain range is known as the "American Alps" and is the home to Mount Rainier?

A: Cascade Mountain Range

Q: What is the only desert in the United States to not have cold winters?

A: The Sonoran Desert

Q: What west coast bay is actually a drowned river valley?

A: San Francisco Bay

Q: What river caught fire and led to the organization of the EPA?

A: The Cuyahoga River

Q: Covering ground into Texas and New Mexico, which is the largest desert found in North America?

A: The Chihuahuan Desert

Q: Which three waterfalls make up Niagara Falls?

A: Horseshoe Falls, Bridal Veil Falls, and American Falls

Q: Which famous dam is found in the beautiful Columbian River?

A: The Grand Coulee Dam

Q: At 600 million years older than the Appalachian Mountains, what is the oldest mountain range in the United States?

A: The Black Hills

Q: What connected bodies of water make up the largest freshwater supply in not only North America but on Earth?
A: The Great Lakes

Q: In what city does the Ohio River flow into the Mississippi River?
A: Cairo, Illinois

Q: The Mojave Desert is in what four states?
A: California, Nevada, Utah, and Arizona

Q: At 35 miles long, what is the longest beach in the United States?
A: Virginia Beach

Q: The Olympic National Park is home to what mountain range?
A: The Olympic Mountain Range

Q: What geographical region extends from Canada to Mexico, and from the Appalachian Plateau to the Rocky Mountain Range?
A: The Great Plains

Q: What Great Lake is home to the Saginaw River Basin?
A: Lake Huron

Q: What volcano located in Washington state had the most devastating eruption recorded in North America?
A: Mount St. Helens

Q: What chain of limestone and coral islands extends from Florida to the Dry Tortugas?

A: Key West

Q: Which ecosystem is home to the largest forest of mangroves in North America?

A: The Florida Everglades

Q: Which Great Lake has an average depth of 500 feet and is larger than all the other Great Lakes put together?

A: Lake Superior

Q: True or false? The Grand Canyon has more square feet than Rhode Island.

A: True

Q: Northeastern New York is home to what mountain range?

A: The Adirondack Mountain Range

Q: Which state is home to the expansive Tongass National Forest?

A: Alaska

Q: Where in North America, is the spot the farthest below sea level?

A: Death Valley

Q: What five states touch the Gulf of Mexico?

A: Texas, Mississippi, Florida, Alabama, and Louisiana

Q: What is the smallest Great Lake?

A: Lake Erie

Chapter Six

U.S. Pop Culture

Q: What was the Rolling Stones' greatest hit?
   A: "Gimme Shelter"

Q: What was the first movie that Marylin Monroe acted in?
A: *Dangerous Years*

Q: Tupac and Dr. Dre referred to what pop culture icon in their song "California Love"?
   A: Liberace

Q: What actor had his two most famous movies released after his death?
   A: James Dean

Q: What chart-topping Rock and Roll artist won three Grammys for his Gospel music, but not his Rock and Roll albums?
   A: Elvis Presley

Q: Who directed *Vertigo*, starring Jimmy Stuart and Kim Novak?
A: Alfred Hitchcock

Q: Who was Humphrey Bogart's lead co-star in the film *African Queen*?
A: Katharine Hepburn

Q: An honorary Emmy Award was presented to which first lady?
A: Jackie Kennedy

Q: Jim Henson was the creator of what much-loved franchise?
A: The Muppets

Q: In 1967, at the Monterey Pop Festival, which performer lit his guitar on fire?
A: Jimmi Hendrix

Q: Prior to Nirvana, what "grunge rock" group did Kurt Cobain play with?
A: The Melvins

Q: Though many peripheral and honorary members came and went, what were the three core members of the "Rat Pack"?
A: Frank Sinatra, Sammy Davis Jr., and Dean Martin

Q: Which rapper is sometimes referred to as "Slim Shady"?
A: Eminem

Q: Remembered largely for his contributions to Jazz and Big Band music, what cornet player was known as "Ambassador Satch"?

A: Louis Armstrong

Q: Who played the role of a detective in the 1968 film *Bullitt*?
A: Steve Mcqueen

Q: Inducted into the Rock and Roll Hall of Fame in 1968, what gospel and blues musician was known as the "Genius of Soul"?
A: Ray Charles

Q: What baseball star was married to Marilyn Monroe?
A: Joe DiMaggio

Q: What "crooner" was previously a boxer known as "Kid Crochet" before starting his singing career?
A: Dean Martin

Q: What 1930s, child film star went on to serve as U.S. Ambassador to both Czechoslovakia and Ghana, before serving as Chief Protocol of the United States?
A: Shirley Temple

Q: What film did Elizabeth Taylor publicly dislike, even though it won her, her first Oscar?
A: *Butterfield 8*

Q: In 1973, what singer-songwriter released "Goodbye Yellow Brick Road"?
A: Elton John

Q: Danny Kaye played alongside what male lead in the film *White Christmas*?

A: Bing Crosby

Q: In 1928, Walt Disney released what cartoon that introduced Mickey Mouse?

A: *Steamboat Willie*

Q: Adjusting for inflation, what film is the highest-grossing film of all time with $88 million, now $3.44 billion?

A: *Gone With the Wind*

Q: What Charlie Chaplin film, released in 1931, took almost three years to make?

A: *City Lights*

Q: In 1999, what musician both co-wrote and performed "Beautiful Stranger" in the film *Austin Powers: The Spy Who Shagged Me*?

A: Madonna

Q: Which television show has run the longest in the U.S.?

A: *The Simpsons*

Q: Known for acting and singing, what icon was known as "Ol' Blue Eyes"?

A: Frank Sinatra

Q: What was Andy Warhol's studio known as?

A: The Factory

Q: In 2000, who released the album, *Oops!... I Did It Again*?

A: Britney Spears

Q: What was the only film Paul Newman and Alfred Hitchcock ever collaborated on?

A: *Torn Curtain*

Q: In 1984, who released the album *Born in the U.S.A.*?

A: Bruce Springsteen

Q: What was the first film for John Wayne and Maureen O'Hara to co-star in?

A: *Rio Grande*

Q: What actor took part in USO tours from 1941-1990?

A: Bob Hope

Q: Who starred alongside Katherine Hepburn in the screwball comedy *Bringing Up Baby*?

A: Cary Grant

Q: How many Grammys were won by Michael Jackson's *Thriller*?

A: 8

Q: What singer-songwriter created "All Along the Watchtower"?

A: Bob Dylan

Q: What actress was best known for her role in *I Love Lucy*?

A: Lucille Ball

Q: Freddie Mercury is perhaps known best for what song, set up like a mock opera?

A: "Bohemian Rhapsody"

Q: In what film did Clint Eastwood star alongside Meryl Streep?

A: *The Bridges of Madison County*

Chapter Seven

References

2Pac-California Love lyrics. (n.d.). https://lyricstranslate.com/en/2Pac-California-Love-lyrics.html

6 june 1944: D-Day. (n.d.). https://www.liberationroute.com/stories/124/d-day?gclid=Cj0KCQiA6rCgBhDVARIsAK1kGPLF0w5O21abGYhN-WCDsc7ejKvsRu6CuEZpgQgggywY1IqnCxJrXaMaAhEzEALw_wcB

10 birthday facts about President Herbert Hoover. (n.d.). National Constitution Center – constitutioncenter.org . https://constitutioncenter.org/blog/10-fascinating-birthday-facts-about-president-herbert-hoover

10 facts about President George H.W. Bush for his 93rd birthday. (n.d.). National Constitution Center–constitutioncenter.org . https://constitutioncenter.org/blog/10-birthday-facts-about-president-george-h-w-bush

10 Facts: The United States Military Academy at West Point. (2021, July 6). American Battlefield Trust. https://www.battlefields.org/le arn/articles/10-facts-united-states-military-academy-west-point

10 fascinating facts about former President Jimmy Carter. (n.d.). National Constitution Center– constitutioncenter.org . https://constitutioncenter.org/blog/10-fascinating-facts-about-fo rmer-president-jimmy-carter

10 fascinating facts about President Lyndon B. Johnson. (n.d.). National Constitution Center – constitutioncenter.org . https://constitutioncenter.org/blog/10-fascinating-facts-about-pr esident-lyndon-b-johnson

10 Fun Facts About the Gulf of Mexico. (2022, May 16). Gulf Shores & Orange Beach. https://www.gulfshores.com/blog/fun-facts-abou t-the-gulf-of-mexico/

12 Things You Didn't Know About Death Valley. (2021, September 29). U.S. Department of The Interior. https://www.doi.gov/blog/1 2-things-you-didnt-know-about-death-valley

13 Things You Didn't Know About Grand Canyon Nation-al Park. (2021, September 29). U.S. Department of The Interi-or. https://www.doi.gov/blog/13-things-you-didnt-know-about-gr and-canyon-national-park

79 percent of private industry workers had access to paid vacation in 2021 : The Economics Daily: U.S. Bureau of Labor Statistics. (2022, August 31).

https://www.bls.gov/opub/ted/2022/79-percent-of-private-indus
try-workers-had-access-to-paid-vacation-in-2021.htm

1973, Secretariat. (n.d.). Kentucky Derby. https://www.kentucky
derby.com/history/moments/secretariat

A brief history of hydropower. (n.d.).
https://www.hydropower.org/iha/discover-history-of-hydropower#:
~:text=The%20first%20hydropower%20projects&text=In%20North
%20America%2C%20hydropower%20plants,%2C%20New%20York
%20(1881).

About James Madison. (2023, March 1). JMU. https://www.jmu
.edu/civic/madison.shtml

About Walt Disney - D23. (2018, April 10). D23. https://d23.co
m/about-walt-disney/

Alaska. (2015, August 8). State Symbols USA. https://statesymb
olsusa.org/states/united-states/alaska

Alfred Hitchcock - IMDb. (n.d.). IMDb. https://m.imdb.com/na
me/nm0000033/trivia

All About Maui's Black Sand Beaches. (n.d.). Skyline. https://ww
w.skylinehawaii.com/blog/all-about-mauis-black-sand-beaches

Andy Warhol. (2023, March 7). Biography. https://www.biograp
hy.com/artists/andy-warhol

Arkansas. (2015, August 8). State Symbols USA. https://statesym
bolsusa.org/states/united-states/arkansas

Augustyn, A. (2023, February 16). *Kurt Cobain | Biography, Songs,
Albums, & Facts.* Encyclopedia Britannica. https://www.britannica.
com/biography/Kurt-Cobain

Battle of the Ironclads (U.S. National Park Service). (n.d.). https:/
/www.nps.gov/articles/battle-of-the-ironclads.htm

Bio - The Official Dean Martin Site. (2020, May 2). The Official
Dean Martin Site. https://deanmartin.com/bio/

Bob Dylan Center, Tulsa, OK. (2022, October 11). *Biography - Bob
Dylan Center | Tulsa, OK.* https://bobdylancenter.com/about/biog
raphy/

Bob Hope USO. (n.d.). *Bob Hope.* https://bobhope.uso.org/abou
t/bob-hope

Boxcar-Admin. (2022, January 25). *About the Lakes - Great Lakes
Commission.* Great Lakes Commission. https://www.glc.org/lakes/

Brighton, C. (2023, January 4). *The 10 Longest Rivers in the United
States.* WorldAtlas. https://www.worldatlas.com/rivers/10-longest-r
ivers-in-the-united-states.html

Bringing Up Baby (1938) - IMDb. (1938, February 18). IMDb.
https://www.imdb.com/title/tt0029947/

Butterfield 8 | film by Mann [1960]. (n.d.). Encyclopedia Britannica. https://www.britannica.com/topic/Butterfield-8-film-by-Mann

Charlie Chaplin : Overview of His Life. (n.d.). Charlie Chaplin: Official Site. https://www.charliechaplin.com/en/articles/21-overview-of-his-life

Chihuahuan Desert. (n.d.). The Nature Conservancy. https://www.nature.org/en-us/get-involved/how-to-help/places-we-protect/chihuahuan-desert/#:~:text=The%20roughly%20200%2C000%2Dsquare%2Dmile,eastern%20and%20western%20Sierra%20Madre.

Cichalski, D. (2023, February 8). *Did Babe Ruth actually hit 715 home runs?* MLB.com. https://www.mlb.com/news/babe-ruth-715th-home-run

Civil War Timeline - Gettysburg National Military Park (U.S. National Park Service). (n.d.). https://www.nps.gov/gett/learn/historyculture/civil-war-timeline.htm

Clint Eastwood - IMDb. (1930, May 31). IMDb. https://www.imdb.com/name/nm0000142/bio

CLINTON BIOGRAPHIES | William J. Clinton Presidential Library and Museum. (n.d.). https://www.clintonlibrary.gov/research/clinton-biographies

Colorado Mountains: 6 Famous Peaks. (2022, September 13). Col
orado.com. https://www.colorado.com/articles/colorado-mountain
s-6-famous-peaks

Cyt. (2017, November 24). *Mountains in the United States |
Mountain Climbing*. https://sites.psu.edu/ct27/2017/11/24/the-s
mallest-mountains-in-the-united-states/

Declaration of Independence (1776). (2022, September 20). National Archives. https://www.archives.gov/milestone-documents/de
claration-of-independence

Deduck, N. (2023, January 30). *11 Mountain Ranges in the US –
Highest, Longest & Most Beautiful*. Love and Road.
https://loveandroad.com/mountain-ranges-in-the-us/#:~:text=The
%20Rocky%20Mountains%2C%20or%20the,British%20Columbia%
20to%20New%20Mexico.

Delaware. (2015, August 8). State Symbols USA. https://statesy
mbolsusa.org/states/united-states/delaware

Digital, M. (2020, March 30). *James K. Polk - James K. Polk Museum. Columbia, TN*. James K. Polk Museum. Columbia, TN. https:
//jameskpolk.com/history/james-k-polk/

Donald J. Trump – The White House. (n.d.). The White House.
https://trumpwhitehouse.archives.gov/people/donald-j-trump/

Duignan, B. (2023, March 4). *Joe Biden | Biography, Family, Policies, & Facts*. Encyclopedia Britannica. https://www.britannica.com/biography/Joe-Biden

Emancipation Proclamation (1863). (2022, May 10). National Archives. https://www.archives.gov/milestone-documents/emancipation-proclamation

Eminem. (n.d.). Shady Records. https://www.shadyrecords.com/artist/eminem-2/

ESPN.com. (2023, March 5). *All-time UFC women's flyweight champions*. https://www.espn.com/mma/story/_/id/24149628/all-ufc-women-flyweight-champions

EuroDev. (2023, March 16). *Europe Paid Vacation Days*. https://blog.eurodev.com/europe-paid-vacation-days

Everglades National Park Quick Facts - Everglades National Park (U.S. National Park Service). (n.d.). https://www.nps.gov/ever/learn/news/parksignificance.htm

Facts about Ronald Reagan. (n.d.). Ronald Reagan. https://www.reaganlibrary.gov/reagans/ronald-reagan/facts-about-ronald-reagan

Flight 93 Story - Flight 93 National Memorial (U.S. National Park Service). (n.d.). https://www.nps.gov/flni/learn/historyculture/flight93story.htm

Fort Facts - Fort Pulaski National Monument (U.S. National Park Service). (n.d.). https://www.nps.gov/fopu/learn/education/fort-fac ts.htm

Four Corners Monument, marking the only spot in the United States where four states (Arizona, Utah, Colorado, and New Mexico) come together. (n.d.). The Library of Congress. https://www.loc.gov/item /2011633953/

Fox, B. (2017a, October 2). *Packers vs. Giants in the 1962 NFL Championship Game: Jerry Kramer Does It All*. Bleacher Report. https://bleacherreport.com/articles/961333-packers-vs-giants-in-t he-1962-nfl-championship-game-jerry-kramer-does-it-all

Fox, B. (2017b, October 2). *Packers vs. Giants in the 1962 NFL Championship Game: Jerry Kramer Does It All*. Bleacher Report. https://bleacherreport.com/articles/961333-packers-vs-giants-in-t he-1962-nfl-championship-game-jerry-kramer-does-it-all

Frank Sinatra | Biography, Songs, Films, & Facts. (1998, October 7). Encyclopedia Britannica. https://www.britannica.com/biography/Frank-Sinatra/The-Rat -Pack-and-the-mob#ref1142934

Frank Sinatra - IMDb. (1915, December 12). IMDb. https://ww w.imdb.com/name/nm0000069/bio

Freddie Mercury. (2023, March 7). Biography. https://www.biog raphy.com/musicians/freddie-mercury

From the spitball to Spider Tack: A brief history of foreign substance use by pitchers in baseball - CBSSports.com. (2021, June 17). CBSSpo rts.com.

https://www.cbssports.com/mlb/news/from-the-spitball-to-spide r-tack-a-brief-history-of-foreign-substance-use-by-pitchers-in-basebal l/

Gatti, A. (2021, January 4). *How Many Films did Maureen O'Hara and John Wayne Star in Together?* Classic Movie Hub Blog.

https://www.classicmoviehub.com/blog/how-many-films-did-ma ureen-ohara-and-john-wayne-star-in-together/

George W. Bush. (n.d.). George W. Bush Library. https://www.ge orgewbushlibrary.gov/bush-family/george-w-bush

George Washington's Mount Vernon. (n.d.). *Key Facts About George Washington.* https://www.mountvernon.org/george-washington/george-washing ton-key-facts/?gclid=Cj0KCQiA9YugBhCZARIsAACXxeIYgJG12 NvEdJnxI64lhL_uPCHNX5M24AgHFhfvY4-_mmazW75qq9YaA qRJEALw_wcB

Gettysburg | July 1-3, 1863. (n.d.). American Battlefield Trust. htt ps://www.battlefields.org/learn/maps/gettysburg-july-1-3-1863

Google Docs: Sign-in. (n.d.). https://docs.google.com/document/ d/1rGWcetEjYNL-odItU16shF0aDABjR_qxNMLEAUoB76 I/edit

Graceland, E. P. (n.d.). *Elvis Presley and the Grammy Awards.* https://www.graceland.com/blog/posts/elvis-presley-and-the-grammy-awards

Great Plains. (2019, December 19). American Southwest Virtual Museum. https://swvirtualmuseum.nau.edu/wp/index.php/cult_land/environments/great-plains/

Greene, A. (2018, June 25). *Rolling Stone.* Rolling Stone. https://www.rollingstone.com/music/music-news/elton-john-and-bernie-taupin-look-back-at-goodbye-yellow-brick-road-205112/

Halloran, J. D. (2017, October 3). *The Rise and Rise of the United States Women's National Team.* Bleacher Report. https://bleacherreport.com/articles/1614739-the-rise-and-rise-of-the-united-states-womens-national-team

Hauser, T. (2023, January 25). *Muhammad Ali | Biography, Bouts, Record, & Facts.* Encyclopedia Britannica. https://www.britannica.com/biography/Muhammad-Ali-boxer

Hawaii. (2015, August 8). State Symbols USA. https://statesymbolsusa.org/states/united-states/hawaii

Hidden treasures: America's rainforests. (n.d.). The Wilderness Society. https://www.wilderness.org/articles/blog/hidden-treasures-americas-rainforests

Highest-grossing film at the global box office (inflation-adjusted). (n.d.). Guinness World Records. https://www.guinnessworldrecord s.com/world-records/highest-box-office-film-gross-inflation-adjusted

History. (n.d.). March of Dimes. https://www.marchofdimes.org /history

History of USNA. (n.d.). https://www.usna.edu/USNAHistory/i ndex.php

Holes-in-One: PGA TOUR Media Guide. (n.d.). https://www.p gatourmediaguide.com/records/all-time/206

Hrn, K. J. /. S. T. (2022, June 9). *Flashback: These are the 9 fastest Belmont winners.* Horse Racing Nation. https://www.horseracingnation.com/news/Flashback_These _are_the_9_fastest_Belmont_winners_123

Illinois. (2015, August 8). State Symbols USA. https://statesymb olsusa.org/states/united-states/illinois

IMDb. (n.d.-a). *Lucille Ball.* IMDb. https://www.imdb.com/na me/nm0000840/

IMDb. (n.d.-b). *Marilyn Monroe.* IMDb. https://www.imdb.co m/name/nm0000054/

Indiana. (2015, August 8). State Symbols USA. https://statesym bolsusa.org/states/united-states/indiana

International Bowling Museum. (n.d.). https://www.bowlingmuseum.com/Visit/Online-Exhibits/History-of-Bowling-in-the-US

Iowa. (2015, August 8). State Symbols USA. https://statesymbolsusa.org/states/united-states/iowa

Isham, K., PsyD LP. (2021, June 15). *Importance of taking a vacation.* Allina Health. Retrieved March 19, 2023, from
https://www.allinahealth.org/healthysetgo/thrive/importance-of-taking-a-vacation

It, M. S. O. S.-. (n.d.). *Missouri State Dessert - Missouri Secretary of State.* https://www.sos.mo.gov/symbol/dessert

James, D. C. (2023, January 22). *Douglas MacArthur | Biography, Command, & Facts.* Encyclopedia Britannica. https://www.britannica.com/biography/Douglas-MacArthur

Jimi Hendrix Experience | Rock & Roll Hall of Fame. (n.d.). https://www.rockhall.com/inductees/jimi-hendrix-experience?gclid=Cj0KCQjwtsCgBhDEARIsAE7RYh0vz2NYcjQrKPpkJO112uoZ5Tc77Efff_ZUuCVmTZyo_J3_vIzO3gsaAkUbEALw_wcB

Klein, C. (2022, January 29). *10 Things You May Not Know About Abraham Lincoln.* HISTORY. https://www.history.com/news/10-things-you-may-not-know-about-abraham-lincoln

Klein, C. (2023a, January 24). *Did William Howard Taft Really Get Stuck in a Bathtub?* HISTORY. https://www.history.com/news/did-william-howard-taft-really-get-stuck-in-a-bathtub

Klein, C. (2023b, January 24). *Did William Howard Taft Really Get Stuck in a Bathtub?* HISTORY. https://www.history.com/news/did-william-howard-taft-really-get-stuck-in-a-bathtub

Korean War | Eisenhower Presidential Library. (n.d.). https://www.eisenhowerlibrary.gov/research/online-documents/korean-war#:~:text=Concerned%20that%20the%20Soviet%20Union, of%20Korea%20in%20its%20defense.

La Sala, A., & La Sala, A. (2021, November 5). *7 Reasons You Should Exercise During the Holidays.* EōS Fitness. https://eosfitness.com/blog/7-reasons-you-should-exercise-during-the-holidays/

Laub, Z. (2017, May 1). *The U.S. War in Afghanistan.* Council on Foreign Relations. https://www.cfr.org/timeline/us-war-afghanistan

Lexington and Concord. (n.d.). American Battlefield Trust. https://www.battlefields.org/learn/videos/lexington-and-concord?ms=googlegrant

Life of Jacqueline B. Kennedy | JFK Library. (n.d.). https://www.jfklibrary.org/learn/about-jfk/life-of-jacqueline-b-kennedy

Lineberry, C. (2007, March 1). *The Story Behind the Star Spangled Banner.* Smithsonian Magazine. https://www.smithsonianmag.com/history/the-story-behind-the-star-spangled-banner-149220970/

Longest Beach in the USA. (n.d.). https://www.pacific-coast-high way-travel.com/Longest-Beach-in-the-USA.html

Longest Running TV Shows - IMDb. (2019, February 19). IMDb. https://www.imdb.com/list/ls043477524/

Louis Armstrong Home Museum. (2022, January 25). *Biography - Louis Armstrong Home Museum*. https://www.louisarmstronghous e.org/biography/

Maine. (2015, August 8). State Symbols USA. https://statesymb olsusa.org/states/united-states/maine

Marsh, D. (2023, March 12). *Bruce Springsteen | Biography, Songs, Albums, & Facts*. Encyclopedia Britannica. https://www.britannica. com/biography/Bruce-Springsteen

Massachusetts. (2015, August 8). State Symbols USA. https://sta tesymbolsusa.org/states/united-states/massachusetts

Maxfield, D. (2018, December 25). *General Sherman's Christmas in Savannah*. Emerging Civil War. https://emergingcivilwar.com/2 018/12/25/general-shermans-christmas-in-savannah/

McNamara, D. J. (2020, February 18). *8 Facts You Didn't Know About America's Everglades — And Why We Must Restore this Incredible Place • The National Wildlife Federation Blog*. The National   Wildlife   Federation   Blog. https://blog.nwf.org/2019/12/8-facts-you-didnt-know-about-ameri cas-everglades-and-why-we-must-restore-this-incredible-place/

Michigan. (2015, August 8). State Symbols USA. https://statesy
mbolsusa.org/states/united-states/michigan

Military Benefits. (2021, July 11). *Presidents that Served in the Military - Veteran.com*. Veteran.com. https://veteran.com/presidents-th
at-served/

Mississippi. (2015, August 8). State Symbols USA. https://states
ymbolsusa.org/states/united-states/mississippi

Mississippi River Delta | National Wildlife Federation. (n.d.). Na-
tional Wildlife Federation. https://www.nwf.org/Educational-Reso
urces/Wildlife-Guide/Wild-Places/Mississippi-River-Delta

MonkEL. (n.d.). *"Grover the Good" - Grover Cleveland's Birthday*.
National Portrait Gallery. https://npg.si.edu/blog/grover-good-grov
er-cleveland%E2%80%99s-birthday

Montana. (2015, August 8). State Symbols USA. https://statesy
mbolsusa.org/states/united-states/montana

Morgan Horse. (n.d.). Vermont History Explorer. https://vermo
nthistoryexplorer.org/vermont-state-animal

NASCAR. (2023, January 17). *NASCAR History | Official Site Of
NASCAR*.   Official   Site   of   NASCAR.
https://www.nascar.com/nascar-history#:~:text=DECEMBER%201
4%2C%201947%20%E2%80%93%20Bill%20France,at%20the%20be
ach%20road%20course.

Nation, N. (2022, February 2). *How did your NFL team gets its name? Origins explained for all 32.* ESPN.com . https://www.espn.com/nfl/story/_/id/32814182/how-did-your-nfl-team-gets-name-origins-explained-all-32

National Park System (U.S. National Park Service). (n.d.). https://www.nps.gov/aboutus/national-park-system.htm#:~:text=The%20National%20Park%20System%20has,of%20current%20and%20future%20generations.

National Steeplechase Museum - Camden, SC. (n.d.). https://nationalsteeplechasemuseum.org/the-history-of-steeplechase-racing/

Nevada. (2015, August 8). State Symbols USA. https://statesymbolsusa.org/states/united-states/nevada

New Hampshire. (2015, August 8). State Symbols USA. https://statesymbolsusa.org/states/united-states/new-hampshire

New Jersey. (2015, August 8). State Symbols USA. https://statesymbolsusa.org/states/united-states/new-jersey

NFL All-Time Touchdowns Leaders - National Football League - ESPN. (n.d.). ESPN.com. http://www.espn.com/nfl/history/leaders

NFL founded in Canton on Sept. 17, 1920 | Pro Football Hall of Fame Official Site. (n.d.). Pfhof. https://www.profootballhof.com/news/2005/01/news-nfl-founded-in-canton/

NHL Records. (n.d.). https://records.nhl.com/history

Niagara Falls Fun Facts. (n.d.). Niagara Falls USA. https://www.niagarafallsusa.com/planning-tools/about-niagara-falls/fun-facts/

North American Deserts. (n.d.). https://www.desertmuseum.org/books/nhsd_northamerica.php

North Carolina. (2015, August 8). State Symbols USA. https://statesymbolsusa.org/states/united-states/north-carolina

North Dakota. (2015, August 8). State Symbols USA. https://statesymbolsusa.org/states/united-states/north-dakota

NSSA Hall of Fame Inductees. (n.d.). https://mynssa.nssa-nsca.org/nssa-hall-of-fame/nssa-hall-of-fame-inductees/

O'Brien, L. M. (2023, February 26). *Madonna | Biography, Songs, & Facts*. Encyclopedia Britannica. https://www.britannica.com/biography/Madonna-American-singer-and-actress

Office of the State Of Minnesota Secretary of State. (n.d.). https://www.sos.state.mn.us/about-minnesota/state-symbols/

Official State Insects. (n.d.). www.InsectIdentification.org. https://www.insectidentification.org/official-state-insects.php

Oklahoma. (2015, August 8). State Symbols USA. https://statesymbolsusa.org/states/united-states/oklahoma

Olympics.com. (2023, February 18). *Mikaela Shiffrin medals and wins: Full list of records and stats of USA Alpine skiing star.* https://olympics.com/en/news/mikaela-shiffrin-numbers-america n-skier-career-records

Operation DESERT STORM | U.S. Army Center of Military History. (n.d.). https://history.army.mil/html/bookshelves/resmat/dese rt-storm/index.html

Oregon. (2015, August 8). State Symbols USA. https://statesymb olsusa.org/states/united-states/oregon

Paul Revere Heritage Project. (n.d.). http://www.paul-revere-heri tage.com/one-if-by-land-two-if-by-sea.html

Pennsylvania. (2015, August 8). State Symbols USA. https://stat esymbolsusa.org/states/united-states/pennsylvania

PRCA Sports News. (n.d.). https://www.prorodeo.com/prorodeo /cowboys/world-champions-historical/

President Nixon | Richard Nixon Museum and Library. (n.d.). https://www.nixonlibrary.gov/index.php/president-nixon

Ray Charles | Rock & Roll Hall of Fame. (n.d.). https://www.rockhall.com/inductees/ray-charles?gclid=Cj0KCQjw wtWgBhDhARIsAEMcxeCacicxDl_WqgtDv_beFBj2qfh_iW-sUlh wDUge22PqXQtgLOkHGt4aAubWEALw_wcB

Rhode Island. (2015, August 8). State Symbols USA. https://stat esymbolsusa.org/states/united-states/rhode-island

Rutherford B. Hayes. (n.d.). American Battlefield Trust. https://w ww.battlefields.org/learn/biographies/rutherford-b-hayes

Safety Tips for Traveling | RAINN. (n.d.). https://www.rainn.or g/articles/safety-tips-traveling

Scancarelli, D. (2022, December 20). *The 10 best Rolling Stones songs of all time.* EW.com. https://ew.com/music/the-best-rolling-s tones-songs-of-all-time/

Shirley Temple - New World Encyclopedia. (n.d.). https://www.n ewworldencyclopedia.org/entry/Shirley_Temple

Simpson, V. (2020, July 18). *Oldest Mountain Ranges Of The World.* WorldAtlas. https://www.worldatlas.com/articles/oldest-m ountain-ranges-of-the-world.html

Smith, A. S. (2018, April 9). *The History of the Football Helmet - Brain Injury Law Center.* Brain Injury Law Center. https://www.b rain-injury-law-center.com/blog/history-football-helmet/

State Bird | Maggie Toulouse Oliver - New Mexico Secretary of State. (n.d.). https://www.sos.nm.gov/about-new-mexico/state-bird/

State Soil - Florida Department of State. (n.d.). https://dos.myflo rida.com/florida-facts/florida-state-symbols/state-soil/

State Symbols – California State Library. (n.d.). https://library.ca.gov/california-history/state-symbols/#:~:text=the%20State%20Legislature.-,Bird,for%20its%20hardiness%20and%20adaptability.

State Symbols - The official website of Louisiana. (n.d.). https://www.louisiana.gov/about-louisiana/state-symbols/

Statute | Kansas State Legislature. (n.d.). http://www.kslegislature.org/li_2020/b2019_20/statute/073_000_0000_chapter/073_018_0000_article/073_018_0001_section/073_018_0001_k/#:~:text=Be%20it%20enacted%20by%20the,R.S.%201923%2C%2075%2D3033.

Steve McQueen - IMDb. (1930, March 24). IMDb. https://www.imdb.com/name/nm0000537/bio

Sudden Death, Assassination Attempts, and Mourning. (2021, June 25). National Museum of American History. https://americanhistory.si.edu/american-presidency/life-and-death-white-house/death

Symbols of New York State - NYS Dept. of Environmental Conservation. (n.d.). https://www.dec.ny.gov/education/1887.html

T. R. the Rough Rider: Hero of the Spanish American War - Theodore Roosevelt Birthplace National Historic Site (U.S. National Park Service). (n.d.). https://www.nps.gov/thrb/learn/historyculture/tr-rr-spanamwar.htm

Tenley E. Albright Performance Center – The Skating Club of Boston. (n.d.). https://scboston.org/performance-center/

Tennessee. (2015, August 8). State Symbols USA. https://statesym bolsusa.org/states/united-states/tennessee

Texas   State   Symbols.   (n.d.). https://www.thestoryoftexas.com/education/texas-symbols#:~:text= The%20longhorn%20became%20the%20large,%2Dtailed%20bat%2 0(1995).

The 1969 Cuyahoga River Fire (U.S. National Park Service). (n.d.). https://www.nps.gov/articles/story-of-the-fire.htm#:~:text=Railroad %20bridges%20near%20Republic%20Steel,spark%20that%20ignited %20the%20debris.

The African Queen (1951) - IMDb. (1952, March 21). IMDb. ht tps://www.imdb.com/title/tt0043265/?ref_=nm_knf_t_3

The Bay of Pigs | JFK Library. (n.d.). https://www.jfklibrary.org/ learn/about-jfk/jfk-in-history/the-bay-of-pigs#:~:text=

The Editors of Encyclopaedia Britannica. (1998a, July 20). *Dry Tortugas | islands, Florida, United States*. Encyclopedia Britannica. https://www.britannica.com/place/Dry-Tortugas

The Editors of Encyclopaedia Britannica. (1998b, July 20). *Ho Chi Minh Trail | History, Route, & Map*. Encyclopedia Britannica. http s://www.britannica.com/topic/Ho-Chi-Minh-Trail

The Editors of Encyclopaedia Britannica. (1998c, July 20). *Mount Saint Helens | Location, Eruption, & Facts*. Encyclopedia Britannica. https://www.britannica.com/place/Mount-Saint-Helens

The Editors of Encyclopaedia Britannica. (1999a, May 27). *Mojave Desert | Location, Map, Plants, Climate, & Facts*. Encyclopedia Britannica.
https://www.britannica.com/place/Mojave-Desert

The Editors of Encyclopaedia Britannica. (1999b, July 28). *San Francisco Bay | bay, California, United States*. Encyclopedia Britannica.
https://www.britannica.com/place/San-Francisco-Bay

The Editors of Encyclopaedia Britannica. (2007, October 3). *Britney Spears | Biography, Songs, Albums, Documentary, & Facts*. Encyclopedia Britannica.
https://www.britannica.com/biography/Britney-Spears

The Editors of Encyclopaedia Britannica. (2022, May 2). *The Muppet Show | History, Characters, Episodes, & Facts*. Encyclopedia Britannica.
https://www.britannica.com/topic/The-Muppet-Show

The Editors of Encyclopaedia Britannica. (2023a, January 5). *Calvin Coolidge | Biography, Facts, &*
Quotes. Encyclopedia Britannica. https://www.britannica.com/biography/Calvin-Coolidge

The Editors of Encyclopaedia Britannica. (2023b, January 16). *Franklin Pierce | Biography & Facts.*
Encyclopedia Britannica. https://www.britannica.com/biography/Franklin-Pierce

The Editors of Encyclopaedia Britannica. (2023c, February 1). *Charles Cornwallis, 1st Marquess and 2nd Earl Cornwallis | British general and statesman.* Encyclopedia Britannica. https://www.britannica.com/biography/Charles-Cornwallis-1st-Marquess-and-2nd-Earl-Cornwallis

The Editors of Encyclopaedia Britannica. (2023d, February 4). *James Dean | Biography, Movies, Death, & Facts.* Encyclopedia Britannica.
https://www.britannica.com/biography/James-Dean-American-actor

The Editors of Encyclopaedia Britannica. (2023e, February 15). *Chesapeake Bay | Location, History, & Facts.* Encyclopedia Britannica. https://www.britannica.com/place/Chesapeake-Bay

The Editors of Encyclopaedia Britannica. (2023f, February 17). *Ohio River | river, United States.* Encyclopedia Britannica. https://www.britannica.com/place/Ohio-River

The Editors of Encyclopaedia Britannica. (2023g, March 4). *Joe DiMaggio | Biography & Facts.* Encyclopedia Britannica. https://www.britannica.com/biography/Joe-DiMaggio

The Editors of Encyclopaedia Britannica. (2023h, March 4). *Millard Fillmore | Presidency, Accomplishments, & Facts*. Encyclopedia Britannica.

https://www.britannica.com/biography/Millard-Fillmore

The Editors of Encyclopaedia Britannica. (2023i, March 4). *National Basketball Association | History & Facts*. Encyclopedia Britannica.

https://www.britannica.com/topic/National-Basketball-Association

The Editors of Encyclopaedia Britannica. (2023j, March 10). *Kilauea | Location, Eruptions, & Facts*. Encyclopedia Britannica.
https://www.britannica.com/place/Kilauea

The   Five   Riders.   (n.d.).
https://www.constitutionfacts.com/us-declaration-of-independence/the-five-riders/#:~:text=Four%20men%20and%20one%20woman,William%20Dawes%2C%20and%20Sybil%20Ludington.

The Korean War Chronology | U.S. Army Center of Military History. (n.d.). https://history.army.mil/reference/korea/kw-chrono.htm

The President - Benjamin Harrison. (2020, January 17). Benjamin Harrison. https://bhpsite.org/learn/benjamin-harrison/president/

The State Flower. (n.d.). CT.gov - Connecticut's Official State W   e   b   s   i   t   e   .
https://portal.ct.gov/About/State-Symbols/The-State-Flower#:~:tex

t=Designated%20as%20the%20State%20Flower,beautiful%20of%20 native%20American%20shrubs.

The White House. (2022a, July 12). *Presidents | The White House*. https://www.whitehouse.gov/about-the-white-house/presidents/

The White House. (2022b, December 23). *Andrew Jackson | The White House*. https://www.whitehouse.gov/about-the-white-house /presidents/andrew-jackson/

The White House. (2022c, December 23). *James Buchanan | The White House*. https://www.whitehouse.gov/about-the-white-house/presidents/ja mes-buchanan/#:~:text=James%20Buchanan%2C%20the%2015th% 20President,to%20remain%20a%20lifelong%20bachelor.

The White House. (2022d, December 23). *James Monroe | The White House*. https://www.whitehouse.gov/about-the-white-house /presidents/james-monroe/

The White House. (2022e, December 23). *John Adams | The White House*. https://www.whitehouse.gov/about-the-white-house/presid ents/john-adams/

The White House. (2022f, December 23). *William Henry Harrison | The White House*. https://www.whitehouse.gov/about-the-white-house/presidents/will iam-henry-harrison/#:~:text=William%20Henry%20Harrison%2C% 20an%20American,tenure%20in%20U.S.%20Presidential%20history .

Theodore Roosevelt and the National Park System - Theodore Roosevelt Birthplace National Historic Site (U.S. National Park Service). (n.d.).
https://www.nps.gov/thrb/learn/historyculture/trandthenpsystem.htm

This Day in History: Four Presidents – and a VP – Received the Nobel. (2015, August 12). whitehouse.gov . https://obamawhitehouse.archives.gov/blog/2014/12/10/day-history-four-presidents-and-vp-received-nobel-peace-prize

Tongass National Forest - About the Forest. (n.d.). https://www.fs.usda.gov/main/tongass/about-forest#:~:text=At%20roughly%20the%20size%20of,including%20the%20state%20capital%2C%20Juneau

Travis, William Barret. (n.d.). The Alamo. https://www.thealamo.org/remember/battle-and-revolution/defenders/william-barret-travis#fromDefendersList

Tunisia Campaign. (n.d.). https://encyclopedia.ushmm.org/content/en/article/tunisia-campaign

Turner Classic Movies - TCM.com. (n.d.). Watch TCM. https://www.tcm.com/tcmdb/person/140544%7C122194/Paul-Newman/#life-events

Ulysses S. Grant | Biography, Presidency, & History. (1999, July 28). Encyclopedia Britannica. https://www.britannica.com/biograp hy/Ulysses-S-Grant/Grants-presidency

U.S. Department of Defense. (n.d.). *Remembering Navy WAVES During Women's History Month.* https://www.defense.gov/News/News-Stories/Article/Article/1102 371/remembering-navy-waves-during-womens-history-month/

U.S. Senate: John Quincy Adams: A Featured Biography. (2022, June 3). https://www.senate.gov/senators/FeaturedBios/Featured_Bio_Ada msJohnQ.htm#:~:text=The%20political%20career%20of%20John,re present%20the%20state%20of%20Massachusetts.

U.S. Soccer Federation. (n.d.). *Timeline.* https://www.ussoccer.c om/history/timeline

USA Track & Field | American Records. (n.d.). https://www.usat f.org/resources/statistics/records/american-records

User, S. (n.d.). *President Martin Van Buren.* https://famous-trial s.com/amistad/1231-ami-bvan

USTA History. (n.d.). https://www.usta.com/en/home/about-us ta/usta-history/national/usta-history.html

Utah. (2015, August 8). State Symbols USA. https://statesymbol susa.org/states/united-states/utah

Vincent, R. (1999, October 28). *Michael Jackson | Biography, Albums, Songs, Thriller, Beat It, & Facts*. Encyclopedia Britannica. https://www.britannica.com/biography/Michael-Jackson

Virginia. (2015, August 8). State Symbols USA. https://statesymbolsusa.org/states/united-states/virginia

Wanamaker, B. (2022a, October 26). *Lake Erie - Great Lakes Commission*. Great Lakes Commission. https://www.glc.org/lakes/lake-erie

Wanamaker, B. (2022b, October 26). *Lake Huron - Great Lakes Commission*. Great Lakes Commission. https://www.glc.org/lakes/lake-huron

Wanamaker, B. (2022c, October 26). *Lake Michigan - Great Lakes Commission*. Great Lakes Commission. https://www.glc.org/lakes/lake-michigan

Wanamaker, B. (2022d, October 26). *Lake Ontario - Great Lakes Commission*. Great Lakes Commission. https://www.glc.org/lakes/lake-ontario

Warren G. Harding | Facts, Accomplishments, & Biography. (2023, January 5). Encyclopedia Britannica. https://www.britannica.com/biography/Warren-G-Harding/Scandals

Washington. (2015, August 8). State Symbols USA. https://statesymbolsusa.org/states/united-states/washington

West Virginia. (2015, August 8). State Symbols USA. https://sta tesymbolsusa.org/states/united-states/west-virginia

White Christmas (1954) - IMDb. (1955, November 18). IMDb. https://www.imdb.com/title/tt0047673/

White House Historical Association. (n.d.-a). *John Tyler*. WHHA (en-US). https://www.whitehousehistory.org/bios/john-tyler

White House Historical Association. (n.d.-b). *Zachary Taylor*. WHHA (en-US). https://www.whitehousehistory.org/bios/zachary -taylor

William Prescott. (n.d.). American Battlefield Trust. https://www .battlefields.org/learn/biographies/william-prescott?ms=googlegrant

Wins and Finishes: PGA TOUR Media Guide. (n.d.). https://w ww.pgatourmediaguide.com/records/all-time/36

Winter at Valley Forge. (2021, August 24). American Battle-field Trust. https://www.battlefields.org/learn/articles/winter-valley -forge?ms=googlegrant

Wisconsin State Symbols | Wisconsin Historical Society. (2012, May 23). Wisconsin Historical Society. https://www.wisconsinhistory.or g/Records/Article/CS2908

Wolf, J. (2017, February 27). *Pierce posts barrel racing record*. Las Vegas Review-Journal. https://www.reviewjournal.com/sports/rod eo/national-finals-rodeo/pierce-posts-barrel-racing-record/

World War II: Timeline. (n.d.). https://encyclopedia.ushmm.org /content/en/article/world-war-ii-key-dates

Written by: Matt Kelly. (n.d.). *The Negro National League is Founded | Baseball Hall of Fame*. https://baseballhall.org/discover-m ore/stories/inside-pitch/negro-national-league-is-founded

Wu, H. (2022). 30 Amazing Vacation Quotes — This Life Of Travel. *This Life of Travel*. https://www.thislifeoftravel.com/resourc es/vacation-quotes

Wyoming. (2015, August 8). State Symbols USA. https://statesy mbolsusa.org/states/united-states/wyoming

Zimmermann Telegram. (n.d.). National WWI Museum and Memorial. https://www.theworldwar.org/learn/about-wwi/zimme rmann-telegram

www.ingramcontent.com/pod-product-compliance
Lightning Source LLC
LaVergne TN
LVHW051159080426
835508LV00021B/2705